How to Walk With The Holy Spirit

By Craig B. Cooper

ISBN 978-1-257-82502-8

Published by Craig B. Cooper

Preface

In March 2006 the Holy Spirit spoke to me with this word:

"The Trinity shall be known in this region. When the Trinity is lifted up the territorial spirits have to fall. Things have to be done in the fullness of the Trinity. 'In the name of Jesus, with the power of the Holy Spirit, to the Glory of the Father'

I felt the Holy Spirit saying that He is left out of most churches. His name is mentioned often but it is usually only in passing. He desires to be an integral and active part of what is happening and not just known as someone that lives inside of us when we became a Christian.

Approximately one month later the Spirit spoke to me again about this same subject. He said, *"Until the people of this region make the Holy Spirit Lord too you will never get the complete victory you desire."* The Holy Spirit let me know that when He is actively sought as Lord too in everything we do then He would move powerfully on our behalf.

When we lift up Jesus as Lord we receive all of the benefits of what happened at the Cross. When we lift up the Father as Lord we receive the benefits that He brings. The Holy Spirit showed me that we need to obey Him too with the same reverence, awe, and submission that we obey Jesus and the Father.

The Holy Spirit is not just a "tag-a-long buddy" to comfort us. He points us to Jesus. He is the voice of the Trinity into our lives. When He speaks He does not do so randomly. He has been sent into our lives to teach us and to show us Jesus. If we fail to obey His voice we will miss out on a full understanding of Jesus and how the rest of the Trinity is moving.

We must make Him Lord in the sense that we pay attention, quickly obey, and follow His leading. He has a role in our lives that is just as important as the role that Jesus and the Father have. If we just casually acknowledge who He is we will not enter into the fullness of what God has for us. This book is to help teach us who the Spirit is, how to walk with Him, and how to make Him Lord in our lives too.

Table of Contents

1

Who is the Holy Spirit?

We need to cover some basics about who is the Holy Spirit. Before we define Him we need to give a biblical definition of God. The following definition is the traditional evangelical definition of God:

there is one God, eternally existent in three persons: Father, Son and Holy Spirit.[1]

The Trinity

When talking about three persons in One God we often use the word Trinity. This word is not found in the Bible. It is a word first used by Tertullian in 220 A.D. to explain this concept. This is the definition of Trinity in the Merriam-Webster dictionary:

"the unity of Father, Son, and Holy Spirit as three persons in one Godhead"

The Bible teaches that there is only one God but there are three different persons in this one God. Each person has a distinct role and purpose. The Bible is clear that the Father, Jesus, and the Holy Spirit are distinct but are also all God.

This concept of the Trinity explains a being that is totally foreign to anything that we have ever seen. It cannot be fully understood with our minds but it is consistent with what the Bible teaches.

In the world there are four main views of God.

1. Atheism

Atheism believes that there is no God at all.

2. Polytheism

Polytheism believes that there are many separate distinct Gods. Hinduism has thousands of separate gods. Many polytheists think that Christianity has 3 separate gods: god the Father, god the Son – Jesus, and god the Spirit – Holy Spirit. Christianity does not have 3 separate gods.

3. Unitarianism

Unitarians believe that there is only one god with one distinct person. This is the belief of Islam and Unitarians. Some Christians have a version of Unitarianism. They believe there is only one God – God the Father. They believe in Jesus and the Holy Spirit but they in different ways are not equal to God the Father. This is not the biblical view either.

4. One God in Three Distinct Persons

The biblical explanation of God is very unique to religions. It is also a concept that is hard to understand. Just because we have a hard time understanding it does not mean that it is not true. Truly our God is amazing and infinite.

Finding the Trinity in Scriptures

The concept of the Trinity was partially revealed in the Old Testament and fully revealed in the New Testament. Notice in the following two Old Testament verses the use of the words one and then our.

Deut. 6:4 Hear, O Israel: The LORD our God, the LORD is one.

Gen 1:26 Then God said, "Let us make man in our image, in our likeness, and let them rule over the fish of the sea and the birds of the air, over the livestock, over all the earth, and over all the creatures that move along the ground."

Here are some New Testament verses assuming the concept of three persons in one God.

John 10:31-33 [31]Again the Jews picked up stones to stone him, [32]but Jesus said to them, "I have shown you many great miracles from the Father. For which of these do you stone me?" [33]"We are not stoning you for any of these," replied the Jews, "but for blasphemy, because you, a mere man, claim to be God."

In *Exodus 3:14* God said His name was *"I AM"* - YHWH in the Hebrew. This name was sacred to the Jews. They never spoke the name YHWH. It was the highest form of respect for God. Jesus used these same words about Himself in the following verses. The Jews understood very well what He was saying.

John 8:24, 28, 58 [24]*I told you that you would die in your sins; if you do not believe that I am the one I claim to be, you will indeed die in your sins."* [28]*So Jesus said, "When you have lifted up the Son of Man, then you will know that I am the one I claim to be and that I do nothing on my own but speak just what the Father has taught me.* [58]*"I tell you the truth," Jesus answered, "before Abraham was born, I am!"*

Matt. 28:18-19 [18]*Then Jesus came to them and said, "All authority in heaven and on earth has been given to me.* [19]*Therefore go and make disciples of all nations, baptizing them in the name of the* (1) *Father and of the* (2) *Son and of the* (3) *Holy Spirit,*

The reason that we need to know that the Holy Spirit is God is there is no need to obey Him if He is not. But if He is God we need to respect and obey Him equally like we do Jesus and the Father.

Roles of the Trinity

Each person of God has a different role. It is important to understand this. As we understand these roles we will understand the importance that the Holy Spirit plays. Many times people think of the Holy Spirit as simply something given to us as a "good faith" gift indicating that we are saved and going to heaven. *2 Corinthians* says this is true but we will learn that He is so much more.

2 Cor. 1:21–22 [21]*Now it is God who makes both us and you stand firm in Christ. He anointed us,* [22]*set his seal of ownership on us, and put his Spirit in our hearts as a deposit, guaranteeing what is to come.*

Let's give an overview of each person's role:

1 Pet. 1:1-2 (NLT) 1This letter is from Peter, an apostle of Jesus Christ. I am writing to God's chosen people who are living as foreigners in the lands of Pontus, Galatia, Cappadocia, the province of Asia, and Bithynia. 2God the Father chose you long ago (Planned a relationship with us), *and the Spirit has made you holy* (Implementing the relationship on a daily basis). *As a result, you have obeyed Jesus Christ and are cleansed by his blood* (We have this relationship because of what Jesus did on the Cross).

2 Cor. 13:14 (TMNT) The amazing grace of the Master, Jesus Christ, the extravagant love of God, the intimate friendship of the Holy Spirit, be with all of you.

Each person of God has a different role with no competition between them. They work together in perfect unity. The Father, Son, and Holy Spirit enjoy perfect oneness with each other. Each is thrilled to help the other display His special glory. The Father has great joy preparing a Bride for His Son, making Him the head of His body, and bringing everything under His control. The Son has no greater delight than pleasing His Father and bringing to Him a vast family of sons. The Son gave his life to fulfill the Father's plan. The Holy Spirit is the conduit of making God's love and Christ's provision known to us.

Jesus prayed that we would have oneness like they have.

John 17:22-23 [22] [23]I in them and you in me. May they be brought to complete unity to let the world know that you sent me and have loved them even as you have loved me.

The Holy Spirit is a Person

If He is a person then we can get to know Him like we would other people. You may be asking, "I understand Jesus who is in the form of a man but can I get to know a Spirit?" The answer is yes! But let's look and see how He is a person even though His form is different than ours.

Psychologists say there are 3 qualities that a creature must have to be considered a person:

1. Knowledge

2. Feelings

3. Will

The Holy Spirit has all 3 of these things:

1. Knowledge

I Corinthians 2:11 For who among men knows the thoughts of a man except the man's spirit within him? In the same way no one knows the thoughts of God except the Spirit of God.

Romans 8:27 And he who searches our hearts knows the mind of the Spirit, because the Spirit intercedes for the saints in accordance with God's will.

2. Feelings

Ephesians 4:30 And do not grieve the Holy Spirit of God, with whom you were sealed for the day of redemption.

The Holy Spirit is sensitive to sin – that is why He is called 'holy'. He is also our friend because He knows how to comfort us. How could He be sensitive and comfort us without having feelings?

John 14:26 But the Comforter, which is the Holy Ghost, whom the Father will send in my name, he shall teach you all things, and bring all things to your remembrance, whatsoever I have said unto you.

3. Will

I Corinthians 12:11 All these are the work of one and the same Spirit, and he gives them to each one, just as he determines (*will* in KJV).

We get to know Him just like any other person. He has a personality and feelings. Remember, we are created in His image too!

Misunderstandings about the Holy Spirit[2]

Misunderstanding #1 – We view the Holy Spirit as a Power or Influence not a Person

The Holy Spirit is not a power or influence that we manipulate. He is not a Christian version of "the force" in Star Wars. He is not a neutral force that pervades all of creation that can be manipulated.

Is this your first thoughts towards the Holy Spirit: "How can I use Him to bring blessings into my life?" Do you seek for formulas and special prayers in order to "move" the Holy Spirit in a certain direction?

We cannot manipulate the Holy Spirit and we shouldn't try. Just as we are not to manipulate others we should not try to manipulate Him.

When we view and act towards Him as a person our whole relationship with Him will change. We don't want to use God we want a love relationship with Him.

It is possible to experience His power but never know Him. He will give you power if that is all that you ask for but realize that you are only seeking His hand and not His heart. He wants a relationship with you. His hand is not to be our main focus. He will bless things because of His mercy but we will only be taking from His hand and not His heart. We want to know Him even if He never gives us anything. If we learn to walk with Him then we will also seen His power in our life. But we want the walking with Him to be the goal.

We want to have an intimate relationship with the Holy Spirit. The Holy Spirit is not just for tongues or power for ministry. He wants our confidence and our trust.

Do you thank Him for the work He does daily for you? Move from a mindset of how do I take from the Holy Spirit and use what He gives me to how do I get to know Him and walk as a friend. One of the best ways to get to know Him is to start telling Him how much that you love Him.

Misunderstanding #2 – Our goal is to get more from the Holy Spirit

The question is not how I can get more from the Holy Spirit. The question is how can the Holy Spirit get more of me? How can I break thru religion, reason, control, and comfort to yield every member of my body more to His will? We need to acknowledge that He is the senior partner and He is to be 100% in control.

When we seek him just as an influence all we think about is how to get more power, influence, gifts, etc. for ourselves. We act like He's a material to be bought and sold like gold.

We need to move from figuring out how to use the Holy Spirit to asking that He use us more! Our prayer should be, "come take more of me". We are not to be focused on increasing quantities or power but growing in levels of intimacy.

If I speak of the Holy Spirit as an influence I will find myself speaking of my gifts, what I am doing, my influence, my ministry, the gift I operate in. We will be in effect saying, "look at my name on my ministry." It always leads to self-exaltation. If we are not careful we think we are something because we have "tapped" into some force or power. We will believe we have the secret.

Christianity is to be a life unselfishly walking with the Holy Spirit renouncing everything of us. It is a life of humiliation so that the Holy Spirit will have more freedom to move through us. We are to realize that we are nothing unless we are 100% reliant on Him. Walking with the Holy Spirit does not produce pride but brokenness and humility. It takes desperate people to walk with God. That is what we need to become.

Ephesians 5:18 Do not get drunk on wine, which leads to debauchery. Instead, be filled with the Spirit.

Filled does not mean the modern definition of overflowing – but means dominated by!

How much of our time are we dominated by the Holy Spirit? What rules most of the time - our soul, flesh, or the Spirit?

Do you try to get Him to do something for you like a magic genie?

Don't wait for the Spirit to fall. Enjoy Him now. Don't see Him as a force to manipulate to get something out of but a person to walk with!

[1] *National Association of Evangelicals – Statement of Faith – www.nae.net*

[2] *I want to acknowledge my indebtedness to Jack Frost of Shiloh Place Ministries for my understanding of these truths that the Holy Spirit is a person and not a power.*

2

Why Do We Need Him?

There is great joy in walking with the Holy Spirit. He truly becomes your friend. You realize what it means to never be alone. Matter of fact, you enjoy being alone because it gives you uninterrupted times of enjoying His presence. He truly is a comfort.

He is also a teacher. He tells you about yourself, others, life, circumstances, and of course more about Jesus who will be our bridegroom. He is a good friend and teacher.

There are many other benefits of walking with the Holy Spirit. This chapter lists a few of them.

Guidance

Acts 13-15 is full of situations where the Holy Spirit lead, guided, and directed the early church Christians. What would our churches look like if we involved the Holy Spirit in our ministry that much? I imagine they would have more life and power.

Our human nature thinks that we have all of the information we need to make the right decision. The reality is that we do not have access to most of the information that we need. We also have limited experience on which to base our decisions. It takes humility to admit this. We will often err if we rely on our own abilities, presumptions, and knowledge! We are not as smart as God. The quicker we admit it and follow the Holy Spirit's leading the smarter we look!

Rom. 8:26-27 [26] In the same way, the Spirit helps us in our weakness. We do not know what we ought to pray for, but the Spirit himself intercedes for us with groans that words cannot express. [27] And he who searches our hearts knows the mind of the Spirit, because the Spirit intercedes for the saints in accordance with God's will.

The Holy Spirit knows the thoughts of the Father and what is best for every situation. He will place God's thoughts in our minds of what to pray for and when! Ask the Holy Spirit what to do! It's fun and exciting!

Strength

Eph. 6:10-12 [10] Finally, be strong in the Lord and in his mighty power. [11] Put on the full armor of God so that you can take your stand against the devil's schemes. [12] For our struggle is not against flesh and blood, but against the rulers, against the authorities, against the powers of this dark world and against the spiritual forces of evil in the heavenly realms.

Satan's power is very real and we must know how to stand against it if we want to see victory.

John 10:10 (NLT) The thief's purpose is to steal and kill and destroy. My purpose is to give life in all its fullness.

We can confront the Devil with the Word of God. This is what Jesus did in the wilderness when He was tempted. When we are tempted the Holy Spirit will bring to our minds scriptures to quote and what other actions to take against the temptation. When we do what He tells us to do it has tremendous authority! It's just like if Jesus said it Himself! We can't fight these kinds of wars with physical guns. They are not flesh and blood battles!

Fruits

The Bible tells us that we need the fruits of the Holy Spirit which are:

Galatians 5:22-23 [22]But the fruit of the Spirit is love, joy, peace, patience, kindness, goodness, faithfulness, [23]gentleness and self-control. Against such things there is no law.

These fruits are the characteristics of a mature person in the Lord. His goal is to make us mature Christians. We need help to become the mature person that Jesus wants us to be as described in *Ephesians 4:13*. You could also call these fruits or maturity character!

Our attitudes and emotions are often like a roller coaster from day to day – sometimes hour to hour! The Holy Spirit brings stability in our emotions and personality by developing in us His fruits.

"If there is one apologetic struggle I live with, it is this question: 'why is it that so many people who talk of a supernatural transformation show so little of the transformed life? Why, when we talk so much about the work of the Holy Spirit in the regeneration of a life, is it not so obvious to the unbeliever anymore, who does not see the change but only hears our language?" – Ravi Zacaharias

As we walk with the Holy Spirit He will bring power to change our bad habits, incorrect thought patterns, and wrong attitudes.

2 Cor. 3:16-18 (NLT) [16]But whenever anyone turns to the Lord, then the veil is taken away. [17]Now, the Lord is the Spirit, and wherever the Spirit of the Lord is, he gives freedom. [18]And all of us have had that veil removed so that we can be mirrors that brightly reflect the glory of the Lord. And as the Spirit of the Lord works within us, we become more and more like him and reflect his glory even more.

It is the Holy Spirit who transforms us into the image of Jesus. The more we rely on the Holy Spirit the more we will become like Jesus.

It does take time to grow fruits. It is no different than natural fruit. A perfectly formed apple does not appear overnight on an apple tree. It starts out as a flower bud and then develops fully. It is the same way with us. But the Holy Spirit is faithful to help us grow His 9 fruits into our lives.

Gifts

There are times in our lives when we need the supernatural to occur in our lives. This could mean we need a miracle, healing, increased faith, a word of wisdom, or Godly encouragement. The Holy Spirit has all of these things and more. He calls them gifts.

1 Cor. 12:8-11 [8]To one there is given through the Spirit the message of wisdom, to another the message of knowledge by means of the same Spirit, [9]to another faith by the same Spirit, to another gifts of healing by that one Spirit, [10]to another miraculous powers, to another prophecy, to another distinguishing between spirits, to another speaking in different kinds of tongues, and to still another the interpretation of tongues. [11]All these are the work of one and the same Spirit, and he gives them to each one, just as he determines.

The Holy Spirit loves us and is faithful to bring into our lives any of these 9 gifts whenever He thinks best. We can rest assured that He has the ability and desire to do what is best for us.

Discernment

As we walk with the Holy Spirit He will share with us what He knows about people and circumstances. This is called discernment. It's a valuable asset because the scriptures say that in the last days there will be much deception from the enemy to get us to move away from God.

1 Tim. 4:1 - 9 (TMNT) The Spirit makes it clear that as time goes on, some are going to give up on the faith and chase after demonic illusions put forth by professional liars. These liars have lied so well and for so long that they've lost their capacity for truth. They will tell you not to get married. They'll tell you not to eat this or that food—perfectly good food God created to be eaten heartily and with thanksgiving by Christians! Everything God created is good, and to be received with thanks. Nothing is to be sneered at and thrown out. God's Word and our prayers make every item in creation holy. You've been raised on the Message of the faith and have followed sound teaching. Now pass on this counsel to the Christians there, and you'll be a good servant of Jesus. Stay clear of silly stories that get dressed up as religion. Exercise daily in God—no spiritual flabbiness, please! Workouts in the gymnasium are useful, but a disciplined life in God is far more so, making you fit both today and forever. You can count on this. Take it to heart. This is why we've thrown ourselves into this venture so totally. We're banking on the living God, Savior of all men and women, especially believers.

The Holy Spirit will keep us believing the right thing when there are many seducing, deceiving demonic spirits operating through people in the name of religion that try to lead us astray.

It is pride to think that we can't be led astray. Anyone can be led astray. Don't get proud or you will be the next Jim Jones or David Karesh. You can be smart and get led astray. You might remember in 1997 there was a group of software programmers who believed there was a heaven in a comet going by the earth? They all committed suicide hoping that they would get there when the comet came by. Only through the discernment of the Holy Spirit can we be kept on the right path, judging rightly, and holding to sound doctrine!

2 Tim. 4:3-4 (NLT) [3]For a time is coming when people will no longer listen to right teaching. They will follow their own desires and will look for teachers who will tell them whatever they want to hear. [4]They will reject the truth and follow strange myths.

3

What is He Like?

If the Holy Spirit is a person then what is He like? Every person has personality characteristics that describe them. The Holy Spirit is no difference. Since He is God He is infinite and we will never know everything about Him. But here are 11 characteristics that we do know about.

Purposeful

Gen 1:2-3 (NASB) [2]And the earth was formless and void, and darkness was over the surface of the deep; and the Spirit of God was moving over the surface of the waters. [3]Then God said, "Let there be light"; and there was light.

We see here at the beginning of creation how the Holy Spirit brought about purpose from nothingness. He brought physical light into a place that was empty and dark. He is still doing the same thing today. He brings spiritual light and hope into places where there is a void and darkness.

As you walk with the Holy Spirit He will show you areas in your life like family, work, etc. that are void and have limited purpose. He will challenge you to replace them with His light and purpose. When you do that joy, direction, and a renewed vigor for life will come.

You can be proactive about ordering your life. Where you know things are not right – maybe even chaotic – talk to the Holy Spirit about it and ask Him what to do. He will lead you onto the path you need to go. He will speak to you! It may come directly or it may come through others, but He will speak to you.

This is why it is important to learn to recognize the Holy Spirit's leading through others. You may be casually talking to someone about your problem and then hear the solution through them. They may share how they solved that problem in their life and while they are talking you realize that the Holy Spirit is telling you to do the same thing.

Whenever you encounter confusion in your life you can rest assured it is not from the Holy Spirit. During these times draw close and ask Him for wisdom as to what is causing the confusion. He is the opposite of confusion. He is ordered, purposeful, and has a plan from the Father to execute. When we are trying to make a decision and there is much confusion we need to step back and ask for clarification. We need to slow down at these times and realize that confusion is never from the Holy Spirit.

Another symptom that is not from the Holy Spirit is distractions. Since the Holy Spirit is purposeful we know He is not wandering around wondering where to go next. One of Satan's primary attacks to slow down the Kingdom of God from advancing is distractions. He is constantly seeking to interrupt and distract us. When we find ourselves being distracted we need to run back to Him for direction.

Part of the key to overcoming distractions is the ability to focus. The devil will often in a church service bring in loud, distracting sounds, constant movement, technical interruptions etc. to break the flow of the order and creativity of the Holy Spirit. Have you notice at home when we are trying to have a quiet time with God, he will cause telemarketers, door to door salesman, and others to call. With the Holy Spirit's help we can learn to focus and ignore distractions.

Restful

Isa 63:14 like cattle that go down to the plain, they were given rest by the Spirit of the Lord. This is how you guided your people to make for yourself a glorious name.

Wherever the Spirit resides there is no rushing around or hurrying. There is rest. Being at rest does not mean we are not doing anything. We can be busy on the outside but restful on the inside. The Holy Spirit is often busy but not frantic. When we are frantic it means that we are out of control or at best trying to keep things in control. The Holy Spirit is always at rest because He has things in perfect control. We need this rest in our lives.

Rest is something that is not found often in the American culture. Matter of fact, our culture implies that we are lazy if we are not always moving! This thinking has permeated many churches. We are often considered "more spiritual" if we are constantly doing something for the Lord.

It is important to learn the difference between busyness and purposeful productive work. They are not the same thing. We need to deal a harsh blow to this "workaholic" behavior in our spirituality. Jesus at the Cross did more for us than we often realize. The key to working productively is understanding that all work with any eternal value is found in *Zechariah 4:6b, 'Not by might nor by power, but by my Spirit,' says the Lord Almighty".*

We need to learn to do only what the Holy Spirit is leading us to do and no more. If we do this we will find that we are enjoying life more and getting more done at the same time.

Don't get impatient and run ahead of God. We usually run ahead of God because of three influences. The first influence is our own desire. We want what we want. The second influence is we are moved wrongly because of influence from others. The third influence is from the devil who wants us to move wrongly in order to destroy and steal from us. Pray about decisions and get His peace before you move.

Phil. 4:6-7 (CEV), "Don't worry about anything, but pray about everything. With thankful hearts offer up your prayers and requests to God. Then, because you belong to Christ Jesus, God will bless you with peace that no one can completely understand. And this peace will control the way you think and feel."

One way we can tell if we are being influenced wrongly by people or the devil is that we feel driven to do something. The Devil *drives* the Holy Spirit *leads*. If we feel we are being driven and pushed and not lead and convicted we are not walking in the peace of the Holy Spirit but the bondages of someone else.

Col. 3:15, (Amplified), "And let the peace (soul harmony which comes) from the Christ rule (act as an umpire continually) in your hearts -- deciding and settling with finality all questions that arise in your minds -- [in that peaceful state] to which [as members of Christ's] one body you were also called [to live]. And be thankful -- appreciative, giving praise to God always."

His direction is the still small voice that gives us an inner sense of peace and rest! His direction often causes us to exercise faith to do it but we know down deep inside that it is the right thing.

1 Kings 19:11-12(Amp), "And he said, Go forth, and stand upon the mount before the LORD. And, behold, the LORD passed by, and a great and strong wind rent the mountains, and brake in pieces the rocks before the LORD; but the LORD was not in the wind: and after the wind an earthquake; but the LORD was not in the earthquake. And after the earthquake a fire; but the LORD was not in the fire: and after the fire a still small voice."

Truthful

Acts 5:3, 9 (NLT) [3]Then Peter said, "Ananias, why has Satan filled your heart? You lied to the Holy Spirit, and you kept some of the money for yourself... [9]And Peter said, "How could the two of you even think of doing a thing like this--conspiring together to test the Spirit of the Lord? Just outside that door are the young men who buried your husband, and they will carry you out, too."

The Holy Spirit loves truth. He is very gracious to those who are honest but is deeply grieved by those who hide their sin!

The Holy Spirit convicts of sin. But if we think we are getting away with something we are actually just grieving Him. It should be obvious that the Holy Spirit knows everything! We need to live as if we are constantly being watched by closed circuit TV. Always walk in truth and you will walk closely with the Holy Spirit.

As you walk with Him He will deal with the "gray" areas in your life. These are the areas where we walk in "white lies" and compromised states. The Holy Spirit teaches us to avoid gray and to be "black and white" in all that we do.

James 5:12 Above all, my brothers, do not swear--not by heaven or by earth or by anything else. Let your "Yes" be yes, and your "No," no, or you will be condemned.

Loving

Gal 5:15-16 (NLT) [15]But if instead of showing love among yourselves you are always biting and devouring one another, watch out! Beware of destroying one another. [16]So I advise you to live according to your new life in the Holy Spirit. Then you won't be doing what your sinful nature craves.

The Holy Spirit always, always moves in love without exception. Love is the most basic attribute of God. He does not have love, He is love. Walking in love is always expected! You don't have to pray about it. If we walk in fear, abuse, gossip, backbiting, anger, and other negative traits it will greatly stifle our walking with the Holy Spirit!

Free

2 Cor 3:17 Now the Lord is the Spirit, and where the Spirit of the Lord is, there is freedom.

We need the Holy Spirit to get free from bondages and sin!

Isa 10:27 (KJV) And it shall come to pass in that day, that his burden shall be taken away from off thy shoulder, and his yoke from off thy neck, and the yoke shall be destroyed because of the anointing.
(Other Translations: 'fat' or 'fatness')

Other words that could have been used for the *anointing* here are fat, fatness, grease, liquid, or oil. What this verse means is that the Holy Spirit will slide off of us our hang-ups, misconceptions, addictions and bondages. This alone is a worthwhile reason to walk with Him!

Walking with Him is the secret to getting free because He will show us how to break the "yokes" upon us. These can include bondages, bad habits, financial difficulties, strained relationships, addictions, fears, depression, anger, and many others.

The following verse is a prophecy about what the Holy Spirit would do for Jesus when He came to earth as a man. We know that the Holy Spirit will do the same for us! It gives us insights as to who the Holy Spirit is and what happens when we make Him Lord.

*Isa 11:1-5 [1]A shoot will come up from the stump of Jesse; from his
roots a Branch will bear fruit. [2]The Spirit of the LORD will rest on him--
the Spirit of wisdom and of understanding, the Spirit of counsel and of
power, the Spirit of knowledge and of the fear of the LORD-- [3]and he
will delight in the fear of the LORD. He will not judge by what he sees
with his eyes, or decide by what he hears with his ears; [4]but with
righteousness he will judge the needy, with justice he will give
decisions for the poor of the earth. He will strike the earth with the rod
of his mouth; with the breath of his lips he will slay the wicked.
[5]Righteousness will be his belt and faithfulness the sash around his
waist.*

An interesting statement in this verse is: *"The Spirit of the LORD"*. Jesus moved in power upon the earth because of the Holy Spirit inside of Him. The word LORD in verse 2 in Hebrew is the eternal name of Jehovah the Lord – The Father God!

You have the Spirit of the Father God inside of You! The Holy Spirit represents the God Head. You can't get any more powerful help and insight than this. You have something even the angels don't have. You have the divine inside of you!

Knowledgeable, Wise, and Understanding

The Holy Spirit has *all* knowledge, wisdom, and understanding. Let's talk about these three things because we often think they are the same thing but they are not.

Knowledge is facts. It is answering the question, 'what is happening here?' Wisdom knows what to do with the facts once you know what they are. It is answering the question, "what do I do now?' Understanding knows why the situation happened in the first place. Understanding answers the question, 'why did the situation happen in the first place?'

As you walk with the Holy Spirit He will give you knowledge (what) of what is not right in your life, give you wisdom (how) on how to fix the problem, and give you understanding (why) of why it happened so it's not repeated.

Getting all three, knowledge, wisdom, and understanding is crucial to learn from our mistakes and to not repeat them again. The Holy Spirit can even give us these things *ahead* of time so that we avoid mistakes. This is the best scenario and often happens when we walk closely with Him.

For example, many people are in trouble financially. To get out of the trouble we need knowledge of what happened to get us in trouble. We then need wisdom on how to change it. Finally, we need understanding of how financial principles work in order to prosper and not repeat the mistakes of the past.

We need this kind of knowledge, wisdom, and understanding in our lives to save us from much pain.

Eccl 10:1 (NLT) Dead flies will cause even a bottle of perfume to stink! Yes, an ounce of foolishness can outweigh a pound of wisdom and honor.

The Holy Spirit is not just for straightening up our messes. He also gives us vision and new direction. He imparts creativity and clarity. He helps us to know how to walk in the future!

1 Chr 12:32 (NASB) And of the sons of Issachar, men who understood the times, with knowledge of what Israel should do, their chiefs were two hundred; and all their kinsmen were at their command.

Dan 1:17 (NLT) God gave these four young men an unusual aptitude for learning the literature and science of the time. And God gave Daniel special ability in understanding the meanings of visions and dreams.

Counselor

Holy Spirit gives you advice for others not just for yourself! Call on it when people need help and ask for your advice.

Strong

The Holy Spirit has the strength necessary to change your life and circumstances. He is not a powerless God. He will give you the strength to do whatever He asks you to do in carrying out the visions and plans that He gives you!

A common tactic of the enemy that steals our strength is fear. Fear enslaves and paralyzes. Pray to God for strength to overcome and not be stopped by inaction that comes from fear.

1 Sam 16:13 So Samuel took the horn of oil and anointed him in the presence of his brothers, and from that day on the Spirit of the LORD came upon David in power. Samuel then went to Ramah.

Humble

Walking with the Holy Spirit will produce the fear of the Lord or humility in us. We are learning who we are, what we can do, and not trying to be something we are not. We are not puffed up with arrogance. A sign of humility is obeying God unconditionally – it is the opposite of pride.

The devil lost his anointing and position because of pride. Since the Devil's fall he has been trying to get us to move in pride too. This is a deadly pitfall that we must avoid at all costs.

Summary

These characteristics are a good starting point of describing the Holy Spirit. I know that as you walk with Him you will be able to write your own chapter of what you have learned about Him. Get to know Him as a person. It is an exciting journey to become friends with God.

Exodus 33:11a The Lord would speak to Moses face to face, as a man speaks with his friend....

4

How to Walk with the Holy Spirit

The Holy Spirit wants to be our comforter, teacher, guide, and friend. But we must remember that He is not our personal servant or 'genie'. He is God. Considering this fact it is amazing that He wants to be our friend and not make us His personal slaves.

He wants us to walk with Him. But we must remember that we are to walk with Him and not the other way around. The next question then is, "how do I walk with the Holy Spirit in the way that He desires?" This chapter will help us get started in answering that question.

As you take your own personal journey of walking with Him ask Him how He wants you to walk with Him. You will be amazed at what you will learn.

Obediently

The Holy Spirit wants to be respected as a person not just considered a force or power. What is one of the best ways to respect someone in authority? It is simply to obey and follow what they say.

Heb 3:7-12 (NLT) That is why the Holy Spirit says, "Today you must listen to his voice. [8]Don't harden your hearts against him as Israel did when they rebelled, when they tested God's patience in the wilderness. [9]There your ancestors tried my patience, even though they saw my miracles for forty years. [10]So I was angry with them, and I said, 'Their hearts always turn away from me. They refuse to do what I tell them.' [11]So in my anger I made a vow: 'They will never enter my place of rest.'" [12]Be careful then, dear friends. Make sure that your own hearts are not evil and unbelieving, turning you away from the living God."

Look at what verse 10 says, *"They refuse to do what I tell them."* Amazing! The Holy Spirit was asking them to do something and they wouldn't do it.

If the President of your country or company asked you to do something you would listen closely, ask questions, and then do it to the best of your ability. This is obedience generated from respect of the person's position.

We are to have this same attitude with the Holy Spirit. We are to respect Him shown by our obedience. This means listen closely, ask questions, and then do whatever He asks to the best of your ability.

Don't treat the Holy Spirit's requests as suggestions or something to do when it is convenient. This is disrespectful and disobedient.

Jesus respected and submitted Himself to the Holy Spirit.

Mat 3:13-17; 4:1 (NLT) [13]Then Jesus went from Galilee to the Jordan River to be baptized by John. [14]But John didn't want to baptize him. "I am the one who needs to be baptized by you," he said, "so why are you coming to me?" [15]But Jesus said, "It must be done, because we must do everything that is right." So then John baptized him. [16]After his baptism, as Jesus came up out of the water, the heavens were opened and he saw the Spirit of God descending like a dove and settling on him. (He allowed the Holy Spirit to come upon Him) [17]And a voice from heaven said, "This is my beloved Son, and I am fully pleased with him. [1]Then Jesus was led out into the wilderness by the Holy Spirit to be tempted there by the Devil. (He allowed Himself to be led by the Holy Spirit – this is trusting God.)

As we follow Him we are walking as supernatural people. We become people not led by what we see in the natural – newspapers, money, bosses, spouses, circumstances, etc. We are led by something beyond the natural, something supernatural, the Holy Spirit!

The Apostle Paul leaned totally upon the direction of the Holy Spirit.

Acts 16:6-11 [6]Paul and his companions traveled throughout the region of Phrygia and Galatia, having been kept by the Holy Spirit from preaching the word in the province of Asia. [7]When they came to the border of Mysia, they tried to enter Bithynia, but the Spirit of Jesus would not allow them to. [8]So they passed by Mysia and went down to Troas. [9] During the night Paul had a vision of a man of Macedonia standing and begging him, "Come over to Macedonia and help us." [10]After Paul had seen the vision, we got ready at once to leave for Macedonia, concluding that God had called us to preach the gospel to them. [11]From Troas we put out to sea and sailed straight for Samothrace, and the next day on to Neapolis.

A sign that we are true sons of God – not just in name only – is that we are led by the Holy Spirit.

Rom 8:14 because those who are led by the Spirit of God are sons of God.

You can insult, make angry, grieve, and test the Holy Spirit when you do not obey and respect Him!

One of the fruits of the Holy Spirit found in *Galatians 5:22-23* is patience. That is because He is patient. But that does not mean His patience has infinite mercy. Don't act carelessly towards the Holy Spirit as if He is not there. He is God and will not be treated that way forever. He can be insulted and enraged. It is a very serious thing to treat the things of God as though they are worth very little. We do this when we don't take seriously what He is saying to us. Eventually, the Holy Spirit demands holiness and obedience. If we don't obey Him then eventually we will suffer the consequences of not walking with Him.

Heb 10:28-29 (NLT) 28Anyone who refused to obey the law of Moses was put to death without mercy on the testimony of two or three witnesses. 29Think how much more terrible the punishment will be for those who have trampled on the Son of God and have treated the blood of the covenant as if it were common and unholy. Such people have insulted and enraged the Holy Spirit who brings God's mercy to his people.

The Holy Spirit can be grieved. This means that He is made sorrowful.

Isa 63:9-10 (NLT) 9In all their suffering he also suffered, and he personally rescued them. In his love and mercy he redeemed them. He lifted them up and carried them through all the years. 10But they rebelled against him and grieved his Holy Spirit. That is why he became their enemy and fought against them.

We are not to test the Spirit's patience and mercy hoping that He will overlook our sin one more time.

Acts 5:1-10 (NLT) 1There was also a man named Ananias who, with his wife, Sapphira, sold some property. 2He brought part of the money to the apostles, but he claimed it was the full amount. His wife had agreed to this deception. 3Then Peter said, "Ananias, why has Satan filled your heart? You lied to the Holy Spirit, and you kept some of the money for yourself. 4The property was yours to sell or not sell, as you wished. And after selling it, the money was yours to give away. How could you do a thing like this? You weren't lying to us but to God." 5As soon as Ananias heard these words, he fell to the floor and died. Everyone who heard about it was terrified. 6Then some young men wrapped him in a sheet and took him out and buried him. 7About three hours later his wife came in, not knowing what had happened. [8]Peter asked her, "Was this the price you and your husband received for your land?" "Yes," she replied, "that was the price." [9]And Peter said, "How could the two of you even think of doing a thing like this--conspiring together to test the Spirit of the Lord? Just outside that door are the young men who buried your husband, and they will carry you out, too." [10]Instantly, she fell to the floor and died. When the young men came in and saw that she was dead, they carried her out and buried her beside her husband.

There is a fine line of relating to God. God is a longsuffering God who loves us. This is true without a doubt or a debate. But you can try the patience of the Holy Spirit. Ananias and Sapphira did not respect Him enough to treat Him with the respect He deserves.

Don't have an attitude that wants to see how far the rubber band can be stretched before it will break with the Holy Spirit. This attitude tries to get away with as much as possible before there are consequences. This is a dangerous game because you never know when the rubber band will break. Instead of stretching the rubber band run towards the Holy Spirit!

It is easy to fear the Holy Spirit as many do by reading these verses. But if you walk closely with the Holy Spirit you will find that there is no fear but perfect love. He created you for fellowship and that is His desire. But He does not want you to commit your affections to another thing.

The Israelites walking in the desert with Moses give us some good lessons about walking with the Holy Spirit. As they were led by the cloud by day and the fire by Night these were signs of the Holy Spirit's presence. We have the Holy Spirit inside of us day and night to give us guidance.

But over time the Israelites grew familiar with the Holy Spirit (through the cloud and fire) that they began to take Him for granted. We as Christians often find ourselves falling into the same pattern. We will say something like, "oh well, I have the Holy Spirit, it's no big deal! I don't need to ask His advice today I will do it tomorrow."

In Isaiah 63:10 the word *rebelled* is used. What a strong word. When we disregard the Holy Spirit and His leading it is called rebellion.

Eph 4:30 And do not grieve the Holy Spirit of God, with whom you were sealed for the day of redemption.

Anything that grieves the Holy Spirit is sin. Ultimately, all sin is a result of not following Him. This concept separates us from religion. Religion is a list of do's and don'ts! But Christianity is a conscious reflection of walking through the day relying on the Holy Spirit.

Another way of quenching the Holy Spirit is to despise the gifts He bring us! The Holy Spirit brings 9 fruits and 9 gifts to us.

Galatians 5:22-23 [22]But the fruit of the Spirit is love, joy, peace, patience, kindness, goodness, faithfulness, [23]gentleness and self-control. Against such things there is no law.

I Corinthians 12:7-11 [7]Now to each one the manifestation of the Spirit is given for the common good. [8]To one there is given through the Spirit the message of wisdom, to another the message of knowledge by means of the same Spirit, [9]to another faith by the same Spirit, to another gifts of healing by that one Spirit, [10]to another miraculous powers, to another prophecy, to another distinguishing between spirits, to another speaking in different kinds of tongues, and to still another the interpretation of tongues. [11]All these are the work of one and the same Spirit, and he gives them to each one, just as he determines.

Every Christian I have met desires the fruits of the Holy Spirit. But it is amazing how many Christians don't want the Holy Spirit's gifts. Think about it, if you went up to someone you cared deeply about and gave them a gift and they rejected it and said they didn't want it how would you feel?

Whole groups of Christian do this every day! They pick and choose which 'gifts' are for today and that *they will allow*. When we reject His gifts this is a personal affront to Him and grieves Him.

1 Th 5:19-20 (NASB) "Do not quench the Spirit; do not despise prophetic utterances."

Gratefully

Psa 78:11-21;40 - 41 (NLT) [11]They forgot what he had done-- the wonderful miracles he had shown them, [12]the miracles he did for their ancestors in Egypt, on the plain of Zoan. [13]For he divided the sea

before them and led them through! The water stood up like walls
beside them! [14]In the daytime he led them by a cloud, and at night by
a pillar of fire. [15]He split open the rocks in the wilderness to give them
plenty of water, as from a gushing spring. [16]He made streams pour
from the rock, making the waters flow down like a river! [17]Yet they
kept on with their sin, rebelling against the Most High in the desert.
[18]They willfully tested God in their hearts, demanding the foods they
craved. [19]They even spoke against God himself, saying, "God can't
give us food in the desert. [20]Yes, he can strike a rock so water gushes
out, but he can't give his people bread and meat." [21]When the LORD
heard them, he was angry. The fire of his wrath burned against Jacob.
Yes, his anger rose against Israel," ... [40]"Oh, how often they rebelled
against him in the desert and grieved his heart in the wilderness.
[41]Again and again they tested God's patience and frustrated the Holy
One of Israel.

Gratitude is one of the keys to walking with the Holy Spirit and enjoying life! Don't be like the Israelites. Be one of thankfulness no matter where you are. There is always something for which we can be thankful. We grieve the Holy Spirit when we do not walk in thankfulness. Be thankful even during the challenging periods in your life.

This doesn't mean that we ignore our problems. But complaining about them is counterproductive. Go with an attitude of faith to God and tell Him what your problems are and ask for help and wisdom. The worst thing we can do is blame God for our problems.

Problems come because we live in a fallen sinful world. They do not come from God. Our wrong actions and other people's wrong actions cause a chain of events that bring chaos and death. God is the only one who can bring true life and start reversing the results of sin.

John 10:10 The thief comes only to steal and kill and destroy; I have come that they may have life, and have it to the full.

Humbly

James 4:5-8a (NLT) [5]What do you think the Scriptures mean when
they say that the Holy Spirit, whom God has placed within us,
jealously longs for us to be faithful? [6]He gives us more and more
strength to stand against such evil desires. As the Scriptures say,
"God sets himself against the proud, but he shows favor to the
humble." [7]So humble yourselves before God. Resist the Devil, and he

will flee from you. [8]Draw close to God, and God will draw close to you...

We saw in the last chapter that walking with the Holy Spirit brings humility. This is one characteristic that as we walk in helps us to hear His voice. The Holy Spirit only walks as a friend with those who are humble and submitted. Someone with a proud spirit can never walk with God! Pride was the original sin that produced the rebellion in the Devil that got him kicked out of heaven. As *verse 7* says *"humble yourselves"*!

Conclusion

Get to know the Holy Spirit as a person. When we approach Him with this thought what is discussed in this chapter will happen. But when we start acting like He is an impersonal force or someone to get something from then we start mistreating Him with disrespect, pride, and manipulation. As you start a friendship with the Holy Spirit like you would with a human being you will be amazed at the fulfillment that will come.

5

Steps To Make Him Lord

The goal of this book is for you to have a great relationship with the Holy Spirit. To do this we must make Him Lord of our life. In this chapter we explore some practical ways to make Him Lord.

Give Him Permission to Move in Your Life

How do I do this? Here are some practical ideas:

- Tell Him right now that He has permission to freely move in you, your family, job, church, business, etc. as He sees fit.

- Tell Him that you will not try to control Him, slow Him down, or stop Him.

- Tell Him that you do trust Him but you will need strength at different times to not panic or take things back into your hands.

- Tell Him that you do believe that He loves you unconditionally and will only do the best for you.

- Thank Him that He will change your life for the good.

- Give Him permission to proceed at whatever speed He thinks best.

- Thank Him for His mercy, grace, and strength.

- Thank Him that He only has your best interests at heart!

Will you honestly answer this question, "Do you think you know what is best for you or does the Holy Spirit know what is best for you?" Depending on how you answer this will determine if He is Lord or not.

Making Him Lord means that He is in control. As long as we hold on to control in some area then we are lord in that area. Making Him Lord is often a scary thing to do. We are putting our faith in something that we can't see the outcome. We are saying that I trust the Godhead more than I trust my own abilities. We know that we can trust God intellectually but when it comes to day to day living we have trouble walking this truth out.

2 Cor. 5:7 We live by faith, not by sight.

It is very hard to live by faith and not our 5 senses and experiences. God will use our experiences but there is a moment in every Christian's life where they have to walk by faith. Faith is simply believing that what God said He would do He will do.

Hebrews 11:1 Now faith is being sure of what we hope for and certain of what we do not see.

This is a hallmark of the Christian life. It says that we believe in something bigger than ourselves.

Hebrews 11:6 And without faith it is impossible to please God, because anyone who comes to him must believe that he exists and that he rewards those who earnestly seek him.

Learn to Hear the Holy Spirit's Voice

There are at least 9 ways to communicate with God. These 9 ways of communication are listed here and briefly discussed from lower to higher order—or more subjective to more objective. Any of these levels can be used by the Holy Spirit to communicate with us.

1. Impression

An impression can best be described by the phrase, *"I feel..."*. A practical example is when somebody comes to your mind that you *feel* led to pray for or call, etc. This is entry level prophetic revelation but does not imply that it is insignificant. Many times in an impression we know something is happening or has happened but we don't know what it is. We don't need to ignore these impressions but ask the right questions to others or the Holy Spirit to try to get all of the answers.

Luke 8:45-46 [45]"Who touched me?" Jesus asked. When they all denied it, Peter said, "Master, the people are crowding and pressing against you." [46]But Jesus said, "Someone touched me; I know that power has gone out from me."

2. God's Voice in Our Spirit

God very rarely speaks to us loudly. He usually speaks very softly. We have to learn to quiet ourselves and pay attention to that small voice or it will be crowded out with other noises. God does this so that we learn to walk with Him intimately as a close friend. Friends don't have to yell at each other. They can communicate with just a look and body language. Train your "spirit ear" to always be ready for a quiet word from the Lord.

1 Kin. 19:12-13 [12]After the earthquake came a fire, but the LORD was not in the fire. And after the fire came a gentle whisper. [13]When Elijah heard it, he pulled his cloak over his face and went out and stood at the mouth of the cave. Then a voice said to him, "What are you doing here, Elijah?"

God's voice is a quiet voice down inside of us that does not come from our mind but from the Spirit. You have to pay attention to listen to it. It is not loud and you can miss it if you're not listening.

Isa. 30:21 Whether you turn to the right or to the left, your ears will hear a voice behind you, saying, "This is the way; walk in it."

Psa. 46:10a "Be still, and know that I am God;…

Many people don't think God speaks to them. This is not true. If you are a child of God He is speaking to you (*Romans 8:14*). Actually He is speaking to you a lot. The problem is not whether He is speaking to you but in us recognizing His voice.

Most people never realize God is speaking to Him because there mind is so cluttered that the soft voice of the Lord is never recognized. Everyone is getting many impressions and words spoken to them by God.

The only way you can unclutter your mind is to unclutter a portion of your schedule. It is crucial that every believer take some time every day and clear off your schedule, to do list, activities, etc. and get into the presence of God. If you will do this on a regular basis you will become still long enough to recognize that God is speaking to you.

After you learn what His voice sounds like and His impressions feel like you will be able to learn how to take this "uncluttered" state into the rest of your day. But you have to learn His voice first so that you can recognize above all the other "voices" that speak to you during the day.

3. Internal Vision

When we say vision we literally mean a picture or a series of pictures that would look like a short video. An internal vision is where you see the picture(s) in your mind. It's just like when you remember an event in the past and you can see it clearly as if you were there. The picture is in your mind but does not affect your sight or hearing of the outside world.

Acts 2:17 "'In the last days, God says, I will pour out my Spirit on all people. Your sons and daughters will prophesy, your young men will see visions, your old men will dream dreams.

Acts 9:10-12 10In Damascus there was a disciple named Ananias. The Lord called to him in a vision, "Ananias!" "Yes, Lord," he answered.

11The Lord told him, "Go to the house of Judas on Straight Street and ask for a man from Tarsus named Saul, for he is praying. 12In a vision he has seen a man named Ananias come and place his hands on him to restore his sight."

4. External Vision

An external vision is the same as an internal vision but you see the picture(s) out in front of you just like you watch a movie or look at a photo. You are still aware of what is going on around you. It is just like if you are looking at a photo or a movie you realize who else is in the room and what they are doing.

5. Dream

A dream is just like a vision except that you get it while you are asleep. Many dreams are literal, but just as often they are symbolic. Symbolic dreams need to be interpreted by someone who has experience and the anointing to do so.

Matt. 1:20 But after he had considered this, an angel of the Lord appeared to him in a dream and said, "Joseph son of David, do not be afraid to take Mary home as your wife, because what is conceived in her is from the Holy Spirit.

6. Trance

A vision where you are so caught up in the Spirit you are not aware of what is going on around you and don't know where you are. It is like you are in the photo or movie and do not know what is going on around you. Many times when you come out of the trance you do not realize how much time has passed or even where you are.

Apostle Peter's experience: *Acts 11:4-5a [4]Peter began and explained everything to them precisely as it had happened: [5]"I was in the city of Joppa praying, and in a trance I saw a vision….*

Apostle John's experience: *Rev. 9:17a The horses and riders I saw in my vision looked like this...*

Apostle Paul's experience:

2 Cor. 12:1-4 [1]I must go on boasting. Although there is nothing to be gained, I will go on to visions and revelations from the Lord. [2]I know a man in Christ who fourteen years ago was caught up to the third heaven. Whether it was in the body or out of the body I do not know—God knows. [3]And I know that this man—whether in the body or apart from the body I do not know, but God knows—[4]was caught up to paradise. He heard inexpressible things, things that man is not permitted to tell.

7. Angelic Visitation

In the Bible when angels showed up it meant they were bringing a very important message for a crucial time. If you get an angelic visitation it is extremely important to consider their words carefully.

For God to dispatch an angel to you means He does not want you to misunderstand or treat the message casually and He wants your undivided attention. Give it. Usually in Scripture when an angel visits time is of the essence. Quickly do whatever the angel of the Lord says.

Acts 12:6-7 [6]The night before Herod was to bring him to trial, Peter was sleeping between two soldiers, bound with two chains, and sentries stood guard at the entrance. [7]Suddenly an angel of the Lord appeared and a light shone in the cell. He struck Peter on the side and woke him up. "Quick, get up!" he said, and the chains fell off Peter's wrists.

8. Audible Voice of God or Direct Visitation by Jesus

This is an extremely rare occurrence but not unheard of. The Apostle Paul heard the audible voice of the Lord while journeying to Damascus.

Acts 9:3-4 [3]As he neared Damascus on his journey, suddenly a light from heaven flashed around him. [4]He fell to the ground and heard a voice say to him, "Saul, Saul, why do you persecute me?"

Everything said about an angelic visitation and the urgency of what is communicated, is much more true about the audible voice of God. Where this type of communication is recorded in the Scriptures it always relays a very important and crucial message. Whenever anyone heard the voice of God it radically changed and empowered the person to a different lifestyle.

9. Word of God

2 Tim. 3:16-17 [16]All Scripture is God-breathed and is useful for teaching, rebuking, correcting and training in righteousness, [17]so that the man of God may be thoroughly equipped for every good work.

Timothy sums up the importance of this revelation – it is God Breathed. The Bible IS the Word of God and is to be treated just as if He spoke it directly to us. When we read the revelation of the Bible and apply it to our lives diligently we will be thoroughly equipped. We will be mature.

Quickly Obey

Deut. 26:17 (NASB) "You have today declared the LORD to be your God, and that you would walk in His ways and keep His statutes, His commandments and His ordinances, and listen to His voice.

In the last chapter we talked in detail about obeying the Holy Spirit. But I want to encourage you here to *quickly* obey Him! Don't debate and analyze in your mind what He has told you. If you pick and choose what you want to obey He will stop speaking to you until you do the last command that He asked of you.

We need to obey His voice quickly even when what He asks seems foolish. God is looking for people who will follow Him even if it doesn't make sense to us. This is what servants do!

1 Cor. 1:27 But God chose the foolish things of the world to shame the wise; God chose the weak things of the world to shame the strong.

Sometimes we won't understand why God asked us to do something until we have done it. God will give us a piece of the puzzle not the whole puzzle. Over time as we get more pieces of the puzzle we realize what the whole picture will look like.

1 Cor. 13:9a For we know in part…

Sit Uninterrupted In His Presence

Set time apart to relax and be in His presence. Just enjoy being with Him. Do whatever comes naturally. The main thing is to relax. During this time let the Lord know how much you love being with Him. When you do this you will feel His presence in a very real way.

The challenge during these times is to stop all the thoughts that come into your mind that distract you. Have you ever noticed how when you set aside time to be with God that worries, to do lists, concerns, and unfinished projects come to your mind? Learn to push through these and don't be distracted. Write your thoughts down on a piece of paper if you need to, but don't stop pushing into His presence. This is a discipline that takes some time to develop. I call it the discipline of silence. But it is one that is very rewarding and will produce a peace and rest in your life that is not often found in our society.

Listen

Come with an open heart to listen. Have you ever noticed how people come into the Lord's presence and never stop talking. They are filled with prayer requests and one-sided conversation. When you come into God's presence ask Him something and then be quiet! Expect Him to answer the question before you fire 10 more at Him. You don't do this in conversations that you have with people (at least I hope you don't)!

When you come into God's presence come with an open mind. Do not come wanting a specific answer from Him. Come being willing to hear whatever He may say. You will be amazed at how vast His wisdom is. This attitude is called humility. This is one of the biggest keys to receiving from God!

James 4:6 But he gives us more grace. That is why Scripture says: "God opposes the proud but gives grace to the humble."

When God speaks to you about something don't try to get Him to change His mind if you don't like it. Don't keep going back to get Him to change His mind. God will not change His mind. He will just stop talking to you until you do the last thing He told you. You can go back to Him for clarification but His will is His will!

Be Expectant

Wake up every morning expecting that God is waiting on you to talk to Him.

Psa. 5:3 In the morning, O LORD, you hear my voice; in the morning I lay my requests before you and wait in expectation.

Pray in Tongues

Rom. 8:26-27 [26]In the same way, the Spirit helps us in our weakness. We do not know what we ought to pray for, but the Spirit himself intercedes for us with groans that words cannot express. [27]And he who searches our hearts knows the mind of the Spirit, because the Spirit intercedes for the saints in accordance with God's will.

This is a great way to hear God's voice and know His will. Praying in tongues is our spirit talking directly to the Spirit of God. We may not know what we are saying all of the time but it brings the presence of God into our life. When God's presence shows up understanding and revelation will also come.

Jude 1:20 But you, dear friends, build yourselves up in your most holy faith and pray in the Holy Spirit.

Pray that all "religious mindsets" will be shown and let go.

Pray that all "religious mindsets" will be shown and let go. We need the Holy Spirit to recognize what God is doing. Very rarely can we recognize God with just our 5 senses. The Pharisees did not recognize God in Jesus at all. It was exactly the opposite. They killed Him. We will do the same without the Holy Spirit teaching us.

Bind Up Fear and Control

There are 2 enemies that we face: fear and control. They are powerful enemies that can keep us from following the Holy Spirit.

Fear of the Unknown

II Timothy 1:7 (KJV) For God hath not given us the spirit of fear; but of power, and of love, and of a sound mind.

We can rest assured that God has the best intentions for us. He is going to take us from glory to glory!

II Corinthians 3:18 And we, who with unveiled faces all reflect the Lord's glory, are being transformed into his likeness with ever-increasing glory, which comes from the Lord, who is the Spirit.

Control

Don't control your life or let others do it!

Galatians 3:1-5 [1]You foolish Galatians! Who has bewitched you? Before your very eyes Jesus Christ was clearly portrayed as crucified. [2]I would like to learn just one thing from you: Did you receive the Spirit by observing the law, or by believing what you heard? [3]Are you so foolish? After beginning with the Spirit, are you now trying to attain your goal by human effort? [4]Have you suffered so much for nothing--if it really was for nothing? [5]Does God give you his Spirit and work miracles among you because you observe the law, or because you believe what you heard?

There is much wisdom in counselors. But in the end it has to be your decision. If you make that decision based on what you want or what someone else wants – then the Holy Spirit is not Lord – someone else is.

Exercise Your Spirit

Just as you have to exercise your physical body you have to exercise your spiritual body!

Heb 5:12-14 (NLT) [12]You have been Christians a long time now, and you ought to be teaching others. Instead, you need someone to teach you again the basic things a beginner must learn about the Scriptures. You are like babies who drink only milk and cannot eat solid food. [13]And a person who is living on milk isn't very far along in the Christian life and doesn't know much about doing what is right. [14]Solid food is for those who are mature, who have trained themselves to recognize the difference between right and wrong and then do what is right." (Heb 6:1 NLT) "So let us stop going over the basics of Christianity again and again. Let us go on instead and become mature in our understanding....

Maturity does not just happen! Your spiritual strength is directly proportional to the degree that you submit to God's will for your life.

To Make Him Lord You Must Tame Your Soul

Our problem is our soul. The soul is made up of 5 parts - intellect, will, emotions, memories, and imaginations. This is the part of us that we often call 'who we are' or our personality. Our soul wants to run our life! It wants to dominate everything. This is what it has always done.

When you became a Christian the challenge is to not let your soul run your life anymore but the Holy Spirit!

Rom 12:1-2 "... but be transformed by the renewing of your mind. ..."

We are not to follow our soul anymore. A soul without God comes up with all types of crazy ideas and quickly becomes deceived. A soul left alone tells you to align yourself with planets and wear crystals in the name of spirituality. Our Spirit is to tell our soul what to do not the other way around.

Eph 4:21-23 (NLT) "... there must be a spiritual renewal of your thoughts and attitudes."

The NIV translates this verse as *" to be made new in the attitude of your minds;"*

Your soul will say, "I don't want to read the Word." But our spirit is crying out for the word. It's a battle! Stop battling and say, "soul you are not in control here, my Spirit is. Shut up and start reading the Word." More people need to start telling their soul and body to be quiet!

When you become born again, we realize that there is a spiritual world and it opens our eyes to the spirits around us. We are affected by our own mind but also there are 2 groups of supernatural spirits that can affect us. The first group is God and His Angels and the second group is the Devil and his angels called Demons.

Eph 6:12 (NLT) "For we are not fighting against people made of flesh and blood, but against the evil rulers and authorities of the unseen world, against those mighty powers of darkness who rule this world, and against wicked spirits in the heavenly realms."

It is important to walk with the Holy Spirit because He will protect us from the influence of the devil and his demons. Before you are a Christian your spirit is dead to God. But it can sense things in the spirit realm if you open yourself up to it.

You can open yourself up to the supernatural demonic realm if you involve yourself with psychics, necromancers, occultists, and other ritualists. This is why the Bible tells us to stay away from people practicing supernatural power from the demonic realm. This kind of influence may be fun at first but leads to bondage in the end.

Deut 18:10-11 (NLT) [10].... And do not let your people practice fortune-telling or sorcery, or allow them to interpret omens, or engage in witchcraft, [11]or cast spells, or function as mediums or psychics, or call forth the spirits of the dead.

Beware of these things because if they are real they are real because of demonic power. But it's faulty, counterfeit, and very limited when compared to the power of the Holy Spirit.

You have been given a privilege as a Christian to have direct access to the throne of God by the blood of Jesus. What the Holy Spirit hears from the throne He will communicate with your recreated, born-again human spirit.

Develop Character not Just Personality

There is a difference between personality and character. Do not mix the two up. Learn to discern the difference!

We all have a personality and we all are to give expression to it. Some people think we need to suppress our personality but this is not true. Some people are dramatic while others are quiet. The Holy Spirit doesn't want to suppress but to inspire and influence our personality. Our personality is to reflect God in every way. But your personality is not the same as character.

What God wants to do is to take your personality and add character to it! Character is when your personality, using it's natural expression, lives out Scriptural principles and laws like self control, patience, integrity, and truthfulness. Character is what gets you through the rough times not a 'bubbly' personality. Character is developed by growing the 9 fruits of the Holy Spirit in your life (*Galatians 5:22-23*).

When you meet a person with a strong personality you may be touched or moved. But when you stand face-to-face with someone with strong character you are changed. Be a person with a great personality *and* character.

How do Christians get in trouble in this area? They follow leaders with strong personalities thinking that it is strong character. Make sure that those leaders you follow have strong character. If they have a great personality then that is a plus.

Signs That Your Soul Is In Control and Not the Holy Spirit

A sign that you are in control and not the Holy Spirit is you are moved by what you want and your desires. When the Spirit is in control you are moved by what God wants.

John 5:19 Jesus gave them this answer: "I tell you the truth, the Son can do nothing by himself; he can do only what he sees his Father doing, because whatever the Father does the Son also does."

Here are some other signs that you are in control and not the Spirit:

- You want to be the center of everything.
- If things aren't the way you like it you get depressed and unhappy.
- If someone hurts you then you engage in self-pity.
- If your soul doesn't like something it becomes rude.

- If you are rejected then you become obsessive or withdrawn.
- If someone else has what you wants then you becomes jealous.
- You to please everyone thus becoming phony and deceitful.
- You do things on your time frame instead of the Lord's.

Your soul is to be harnessed by the Spirit of God and then you will rise to new heights in God.

Mat 22:37 Jesus replied: "'Love the Lord your God with all your heart and with all your soul and with all your mind.'

6

Where is He Taking Us?

Where will we end up if we walk with the Spirit? I don't know the specifics but I can give you the general direction. I can also guarantee you that when you get there you will be glad you made the journey! Every person's destiny has something unique about it. But I will give you 4 broad outcomes that will occur in your life. The specific details will be up to the Holy Spirit.

The Holy Spirit moving in our life can be described as a flow like a river.

John 7:37-39 (NLT) On the last day, the climax of the festival, Jesus stood and shouted to the crowds, "If you are thirsty, come to me! {38} If you believe in me, come and drink! For the Scriptures declare that rivers of living water will flow out from within." {39} (When he said "living water," he was speaking of the Spirit, who would be given to everyone believing in him. But the Spirit had not yet been given, because Jesus had not yet entered into his glory.)

Genesis 1:2 ...and the Spirit of God moved upon the face of the waters.

As we walk with the Spirit we will quickly realize that He is going somewhere and we will need to learn the rhythm and flow of His leading. Flowing with the Holy Spirit is the secret to good relationships, productivity, creativity, power, and faithfulness.

A flowing river is a good analogy of walking with the Spirit. As we walk with Him we are going in a direction. We may not always know the end destination but we know that we are flowing towards something. I talk about four rivers or flows that I know the Holy Spirit is bringing about in our lives and in the earth.

There is no 'magic' number in picking 4 flows. These are just based on my understanding and experiences. But it is interesting to note that there were 4 branches of the river that was flowing through the Garden of Eden. The river flowed from 1 source and then branched out into 4 flows.

Gen. 2:10 A river watering the garden flowed from Eden; from there it was separated into four headwaters.

If I had to sum up in one phrase where the Holy Spirit is taking us it is this: He is preparing us to be the Bride of Jesus forever.

The First River – Righteousness

You are righteous – in right standing – because of God's goodness. This is true because the Father sees us through the payment Jesus made for our sins. The judgment for our sins against God was death. Jesus died for us in our place. The punishment He took was for us. When we ask Jesus to be Lord of our lives then that payment is applied to us.

Romans 6:23 For the wages of sin is death, but the gift of God is eternal life in Christ Jesus our Lord

Spiritually we are in right standing with God when we become a Christian. But our bodies and souls still carry old habits and sins that are not right. One of the major jobs of the Holy Spirit is to bring our bodies and souls into right standing to match the right standing in our spirits.

Why does the Holy Spirit care about this? He wants to make us blameless and holy.

1 Thess. 5:23 May God himself, the God of peace, sanctify you through and through. May your whole spirit, soul and body be kept blameless at the coming of our Lord Jesus Christ.

Why does He want to make us blameless and holy? We are getting married to Jesus Christ! The church as a whole is called the Bride in the Bible and Jesus is the Bridegroom. I don't know how all of this will work out but the Holy Spirit is readying us for a great oneness with Jesus.

Matt. 22:1-2 Jesus spoke to them again in parables, saying:

"The kingdom of heaven is like a king who prepared a wedding banquet for his son."

In Christianity today there is almost no talk about it being like a wedding. God is giving us insight on the truths behind these verses.

John the Baptist, 2000 years ago talked about this subject. *Matt. 3:2-3 (NIV)* describes John's purpose in life

"...Repent, for the kingdom of heaven is near."[3] This is he who was spoken of through the prophet Isaiah: "A voice of one calling in the desert, 'Prepare the way for the Lord, make straight paths for him.'"

John was to prepare the way for the Lord. How did he do this?

John 3:27-29 [27] To this John replied, "A man can receive only what is given him from heaven. [28] You yourselves can testify that I said, 'I am not the Christ but am sent ahead of him.' [29] The bride belongs to the bridegroom. The friend who attends the bridegroom waits and listens for him, and is full of joy when he hears the bridegroom's voice. That joy is mine, and it is now complete.

John the Baptist was preparing a way for the Lord – the Messiah. But look what he calls the Messiah in *John 3:29* – a bridegroom! The parable that we read in *Matthew 22* is an analogy to God the Father preparing a wedding banquet and bride for His son Jesus Christ! Jesus clearly has a bride! This is a strange concept in Christianity today. But this fact is repeated in *Revelation 21:9*, *"Come, I will show you the bride, the wife of the Lamb."* The Lamb is Jesus Christ.

John 1:29 The next day John saw Jesus coming toward him and said, "Look, the Lamb of God, who takes away the sin of the world!

Who is the bride? *Ephesians 5:21-33* talks about how husbands and wives ought to relate to each other. Its subject is obviously marriage. Read this passage and notice that threaded all through this passage is the parallel topic of Jesus and how He relates to His Body. In *verse 31* it talks about two people being one flesh. We know what one flesh means on earth, but look what *verse 32* says this one flesh also means: *"This is a profound mystery—but I am talking about Christ and the church."*

The question then is who is the Body of Christ or the Church? Our answer is found in *1 Cor. 12:27 Now you are the body of Christ, and each one of you is a part of it."* If you are a Christian then you are a part of the Body of Christ, thereby you are the Bride of Jesus!

This is confirmed in *Romans 7:4*. In *verses 1-3*, the subject of marriage is again brought up. But look at what it says in *verse 4, So, my brothers, you also died to the law through the <u>body of Christ</u>, that you <u>might belong to another</u>* (marriage analogy), *to him who was raised from the dead* (Jesus), *in order that we might bear fruit to God.*

What does the Bride look like who is getting married? She is dressed in white and looks as perfect and as beautiful as she can make herself. She has spent a lot of money and time to look the best that she can on the outside. It's a great analogy for what the Spirit is doing in relation to us. He is spending a lot of time to get us to look the best on the inside (and outside too) so that a pure white Bride will be presented to Jesus.

We often think of Christianity as a set of rules to please God. What God is doing is nothing like that. When we think this way we are missing the big picture. The Holy Spirit is not out to get us to act a certain way on the outside. He wants to reverse and change our bad habits and sins so that we are completely new people that *look like Jesus*. He is getting us ready for that marriage. It is all about a relationship and not rules.

All of the things that the Holy Spirit is asking you to modify and change is not just because He wants you to stop them based on some arbitrary standard. He is asking you to change in those areas because He knows what Jesus is like and He want us to look like Him so that we can walk closely with Him.

The Second River – Reconciliation

He not only wants us in right standing with Him and looking like Him, He wants us to be reconciled to Him. What does reconciliation mean? This means we have a great relationship with Him. It means there is no distance between us and Him. We are in a right relationship.

Just as an earthly bride and bridegroom are close and have an intimate relationship with each other the Father wants us to have an intimate and close relationship with Jesus.

We all have a built in desire from God to be intimate with someone and Him. But if intimacy with God never gets fulfilled then we will try to fill it with wrong behavior in relationships or lustful behaviors. When this happens shame and guilt will become a part of our lives.

God wants to teach us how to have intimacy with Him. When we learn to be open with Him then we will stop trying to fulfill that God given desire in the wrong way.

We all long to know and be known by somebody. But did you know that you can do this with Jesus? This is the ultimate intimacy. Just as an earthly Bride and Bridegroom are intimate and share everything Jesus wants to share with us. He wants to be reconciled or brought together with us. If we are willing to be vulnerable with the Lord we can go to great depths of intimacy.

God put this longing in us for intimacy because He wants us to find our deepest satisfaction in experiencing intimacy with Him. God will allow us to know Him more fully than the rest of His created beings. This spiritual intimacy is available to us not just in eternity but now.

The Holy Spirit's desire is for us to get to know Jesus. As we get to know Jesus we will realize that He understands all that is unknown, unnoticed, and misunderstood by others. Jesus feels our pain and struggle. He knows our sin and shame. Yet He believes in us and continues to walk with us.

He wants to share in our victories and prosperity. He knows our true greatness and lives to see us get there. He desires to know the depths of our heart and passions. He wants to be intimate with us in a way that no earthly relationship can. We do not have to be in fear of this type of relationship. Jesus will never violate our trust or use it against us.

Many of us have been hurt when our intimacy with another person was used against us. This will never happen with Jesus. He is trustworthy and keeps secrets! He is only after our best and has no other agenda. He saved you to have a relationship with you – a reconciled one – an intimate one.

The Third River - Revelation

The Holy Spirit wants to reveal to us more about Jesus. He wants us to look like Him, be intimate with Him, and to know Him. The job of the Holy Spirit is to reveal to us more about Jesus so that we can know Him better.

Ephesians 1:17 I keep asking that the God of our Lord Jesus Christ, the glorious Father, may give you the <u>Spirit</u> of wisdom and revelation, so that you may <u>know him better</u>.

As we walk with the Holy Spirit He will teach us things from the Bible that will help us know Jesus better. He wants us to understand all parts of His character and personality. The Spirit is truly our teacher.

The Fourth River – Revival

2 Peter 3:9 The Lord is not slow in keeping his promise, as some understand slowness. He is patient with you, not wanting anyone to perish, but everyone to come to repentance.

There is a lot of talk about saving the world. This is a great thing to talk about. It is what the Holy Spirit is talking about. But have you ever asked the question why does the Holy Spirit want to save the world? Most people will say so that people will not go to Hell but heaven. This is true but why does God want people to go to heaven?

This last question is not as easily answered by Christians. The usual answer is because there will be no more weeping, unhappiness, sickness, etc. Yes this is true. But I propose to you that there is a 'higher' purpose for us escaping Hell. The Holy Spirit is bringing massive revival into the earth like the world has never seen so that the Bride of Jesus will be complete. Jesus wants an intimate relationship with everyone on earth! He doesn't just want heaven full He wants His joy to be full with us!

He is not saving us just to give us a new home and a new body. He is saving us for a glorious relationship with Him. That is why He made us in the beginning and why we will return to Him in the end.

Rev. 22:13 I am the Alpha and the Omega, the First and the Last, the Beginning and the End.

All of history is about relationship. He created Man to have a relationship. He has then spent the entire time since our fall in the Garden of Eden pursuing us and making it possible for us to relate once again with Him. The purpose of the Holy Spirit is to reveal Jesus. As we walk with the Holy Spirit we will greatly appreciate our relationship with Him. But we will find ourselves focusing more on Jesus and falling in love with Him. It is hard for our selfish nature to understand but the Holy Spirit is happy in helping us to pursue our purpose as the Bride of Jesus!

Summary

The Holy Spirit is bringing about 4 broad things in the earth that we are a part of – Looking like Jesus, Intimate with Jesus, Knowing Jesus, and a Completed Jesus with His Bride. Praise God!

About the Author

Craig is married to Susan Luhrman Cooper; a proud Father to Abigail, Grace, and Israel; a Software Developer; and Founder/Pastor of Relationship Church.

You can get more information about the author, his family, blogs, Church, books, articles, etc. at www.craigbcooper.com.

Other Books by Craig

Can Women Minister to Men?

Breaking the Darkness Over Control, Rejection, and Poverty

How to Walk with the Holy Spirit

Faith Fiction

How to Be a Religious Demon

www.ingramcontent.com/pod-product-compliance
Ingram Content Group UK Ltd.
Pitfield, Milton Keynes, MK11 3LW, UK
UKHW041914190726
13854UKWH00003B/1247

9 781257 825028